COPPER THUNDERBIRD

COPPER THUNDERBIRD

Marie Clements

Talonbooks

Talonbooks
P.O. Box 2076, Vancouver, British Columbia, Canada V6B 3S3
www.talonbooks.com

Typeset in New Baskerville and printed and bound in Canada.
Printed on 100% post-consumer recycled paper.

Second Printing: June 2010

The publisher gratefully acknowledges the financial support of the Canada Council for the Arts; the Government of Canada through the Book Publishing Industry Development Program; and the Province of British Columbia through the British Columbia Arts Council and the Book Publishing Tax Credit for our publishing activities.

Library and Archives Canada Cataloguing in Publication

Clements, Marie, 1962–
Copper thunderbird / Marie Clements.

A play.
ISBN 978-0-88922-568-8

1. Morrisseau, Norval, 1933– —Drama. I. Title.

PS8555.L435C66 2007 C812'.6 C2007-901062-8

Copper Thunderbird by Marie Clements was first produced in a National Arts Centre English Theatre / urban ink (Vancouver) world premiere coproduction at Canada's National Arts Centre in Ottawa in May 2007 with the following cast and crew:

THE OLD MAN:	Billy Merasty
THE BOY:	Herbie Barnes
AUNTIE:	Margo Kane
JACK / DR. WEINSTEIN / PICASSO:	Jonathan Fisher
THE YOUNG MAN:	Kevin Loring
THE DUMP BEARS / THE THREE NORVAL WIVES / THE CALIFORNICATION GIRLS:	Renellta Bourque, Byron Chief-Moon, Paula-Jean Prudat
HARRIET / KATERI:	Michelle St. John
Director:	Peter Hinton
Dramaturgy:	Paula Danckert
Set and Costume Design:	Mary Kerr
Lighting Design:	John Webber
Sound Design:	Noah Drew
Projection Design:	Tim Matheson
Voice and Movement Coach:	Nancy Benjamin
Stage Manager:	Louise Currie
Assistant Stage Manager:	Stéfanie Séguin
Apprentice Stage Manager:	Richard Wilson
Consultant:	Crystal S. Parsons
Set Design Assistant:	John Aarmitage

Copper Thunderbird was provided final script development by the National Arts Centre English Theatre with the assistance of

The Banff Centre and Playwrights' Workshop Montreal. *Copper Thunderbird* was originally commissioned by Yves Sioui Durand's Ondinnok Theatre and was workshopped at the Festival de théâtre des Amériques.

Copper Thunderbird Disclaimer

While the play uses 1987 as its point of departure, it is a creative interpretation by the playwright Marie Clements, of Norval Morrisseau's possible musings about his past life. It is not a biography or in any way a complete story of the many complex aspects of the artist's thoughts and history. Rather it is a way of looking at what Morrisseau's work means to us as a country, a nation that is still surviving the collision of first contact over five hundred years ago.

ACT 1

A huge black and white grainy newspaper article fades up. In it, Norval Morrisseau is revealed in a Vancouver downtown eastside hotel sitting on the edge of his bed, disheveled, bloated and alone.

The caption reads: "DRINK OF TEQUILA STARTED PAINTER ON ROAD TO DESPAIR."

And below his picture: "CANADIAN ARTIST NORVAL MORRISSEAU IS SELLING SKETCHES IN VANCOUVER TO BUY LIQUOR. VANCOUVER, 1987."

The black and white newspaper image begins to fade to reveal THE OLD MAN sitting in exactly the same place and posture.

THE OLD MAN looks up ever so slowly, exhausted, as the sky of his room becomes light blue and moving clouds, and he watches oddly as a circle is drawn and hollowed.

A baby boy is released down into the world below.

The baby boy floats down through the clouds and lands into the room as a six-year-old boy. THE BOY appears on the sand of the floor, near the old man's feet. THE OLD MAN looks at his feet curiously.

THE OLD MAN

What now? What are you?

THE BOY looks at THE OLD MAN curiously.

THE BOY

What are you?

THE OLD MAN

" I ... am ... Norval Morrisseau. I ... have ... the Indian name of ... Copper Thunderbird. I ... am ... a ... born ... artist." And ...

THE BOY

You used to draw in the sand on beaches ...

THE BOY begins to print in the sand.

THE OLD MAN

I remember ... I can tell the story ... I used to draw in the sand on beaches. I was six years old, seven at that stage. I drew and if the water came and washed it away ... that's the way the saga goes ... The end.

THE OLD MAN watches with one eye as THE BOY walks toward the edge of the tide leaving behind a trail of boy feet imprints. He stops and turns, waiting for THE OLD MAN to follow.

THE BOY

Are you coming or not?

THE OLD MAN

What do I have to get wet over?

THE OLD MAN laughs at his own joke.

THE BOY goes straight into the edge of the tide. THE OLD MAN watches him splash in and disappear.

The sound of water swirling and filling the room.

The sound of a great underwater world swirls through the room. Cat cries and dogs barking and people talking in strange tongues. Rattles and whispers and deep depth.

THE OLD MAN unsteadily looks at the water and sound that begins to inch toward him like a steady tide increasing its reach.

THE OLD MAN

I drew and if the water came and washed it away ... that's the way the saga goes and goes and goes and goes eh? Where's that boy now? No goodbye ... so much for sad farewells—Hmm ... Sometimes it doesn't matter in this world ... it just doesn't matter ... I wish I could die. I don't care … I don't care anymore because I'd be free. I'd be gone. Goodbye body …

He listens. Nothing.

THE OLD MAN

Goodbye noise … noise where are you?

It is so silent it hurts …

THE OLD MAN

It's too quiet now … why does everybody and everything always go away … Come back now …

He listens. Nothing …

THE OLD MAN

Fuck you then. I'll just talk to myself then …

He tries one more tired listen and then falls back on his bed …

The tide reaches ever forward taking over the room and covering him like a dark blue blanket tucked in to his chest.

THE OLD MAN lies wet, on his bed, face up. He seems to be floating up—suspended. He snores like a bear, muttering, muttering into a story.

SANDY LAKE RESERVE, 1937

THE BOY emerges from the water sitting cross-legged in the centre of a small platform holding on tight to a pet turtle. He lifts the headless turtle to his ear, listening and then talking into its empty hole of a head.

THE OLD MAN

What did you say shell? Come on, echo back a language we can all understand. Come on … don't hide your head my small Mikkinuk … a devil never hides its head under its own shell, or does he?

THE BOY

Are you really the devil with many tongues? I'm talking to you. I can see you. Whisper it through me then from inside. Talk it through me. I will listen. I promise.

THE OLD MAN

Whisper it through me again … I want to feel it. I will listen. I can tell the story … I promise …

THE BOY looks directly at the dreaming OLD MAN.

THE BOY

Then tell it.

Six tall trees shadow up from the water surrounding THE BOY.

THE OLD MAN

My grandfather the most important person in my life. My grandfather the most important person in my life. My grandfather the Mythman. Moses the Mythman took me into the woods straight into the woods and there I was to ...

THE BOY (*this could be spoken in Ojibway*)

... make myself a man.

THE OLD MAN

Make a man of myself. A vision.

THE BOY closes his eyes in fear.

THE BOY

A bear. I can feel a heavy bear coming ... sniffing ...

THE OLD MAN

Is that so? ... Take it from an old man ... whatever you do ... keep your eyes shut ...

A large, black-outlined, vision bear takes shape. THE BEAR walks menacingly closer to the boy sniffing and snorting and breathing.

THE BOY cries out to his Grandfather in the wilderness.

THE BOY

Something heavy is sniffing Grandfather?

THE OLD MAN

He's not here ... It's just me ... an old vision grunting ...

THE BOY

Something coming grunting Grandfather, are you there?

THE OLD MAN

Grunting ... Grunting and hungry ... So hungry ...

THE BOY

... Grandfather please ... help me! It's getting closer ...

THE OLD MAN

It's getting closer this vision ... hmmm ... hungry and heavy this vision upon you.

THE BOY

I'm scared.

THE OLD MAN

You should be scared. Big city visions are sniffing you ... paving a path for you to Chicago, New York and Montreal ... grrrr ... bear visions ... You really want to be a great artist ... hmmm? Then keep your eyes shut ... Like the story goes keep your eyes shut if you want a wish to come true. Grr ...

THE BOY

Grandfather please ... please help me. My eyes are opening I can't help myself. My eyes want to see it coming. I want to know where it's coming from.

THE OLD MAN

Please just keep your eyes shut for once, I'm begging you ... Keep your big eyes shut if you want everything ...

THE BOY opens his eyes wide.

THE OLD MAN and THE BOY look at each and begin to scream in terror. THE OLD MAN because of what he knows and now cannot change, and THE BOY because he looks despite himself.

THE BOY / THE OLD MAN

Ahhhhhh ...

THE OLD MAN

The bear told you not to look. I told you not to look. But you looked because you got no self control. And because you got not self control everything is fucked, everything is half-assed. Nothing is full and everything is half of what it should be. I am half rich now, half famous. I can buy a silver tea set, but I can never have tea with the Queen, understand?

THE BOY understands and looks sad.

THE BOY

I looked because I didn't just want to hear a vision. I wanted to see it ...

THE OLD MAN smiles slowly.

THE OLD MAN

Yes ... yes, I understand ... Keep your head up, it is a royal thought ... Nothing is forever anyhow, ... Maybe we can call Her Majesty the Queen up for afternoon tea, anyways? Hmm?

THE OLD MAN raises his hand and elegantly holds up an imaginary tea cup. THE BOY follows and THE OLD MAN pours imaginary tea out of a royal tea pot.

THE BOY

Two lumps, please ...

THE OLD MAN drops two lumps of sugar into the tea cup.

THE OLD MAN

Two lumps it is ...

Their imaginary tea cups clink in a cheer.

THE OLD MAN

Cheers ... Shake my hand now ... and goodbye ...

THE BOY shakes THE OLD MAN's hand like a man.

THE BOY (*this could be spoken in Ojibway*)

Sorry ... I shouldn't have looked.

THE OLD MAN bear shrugs and lumbers back onto the bed.

THE OLD MAN

Don't be sorry ... It's an old story. The same old story. At least you weren't turned to stone. At least you didn't go hard.

Exhausted, THE OLD MAN saunters back to his bed and lays down falling into a deep sleep. His sleeping man grunts transform as THE OLD MAN finds his penis and begins to stroke himself a hard dream.

THE BOY stands back and watches as—

THE OLD MAN makes a woody tent and it gets bigger and bigger, first naturally and then it grows above everything.

THE OLD MAN becomes shadowed inside. THE BOY draws closer to the walls of the tent. He lifts his finger and begins to draw a black power line on the white tent. He draws the turtle.

THE OLD MAN

Mikkinuk, you turtle you, you devil … leave me alone …

THE BOY

It's just me.

THE OLD MAN

Speak up. Stop whispering … Me who?

THE BOY

You know who …

THE OLD MAN

Why should I care? You're making me all soft here. You are worse than the Devil … you got bad timing … go away …

THE BOY

No.

THE OLD MAN

Then be quiet!

THE BOY

I don't have to.

THE OLD MAN

You don't have to … is that so? What if I made you? That wouldn't work with you would it … What if you made me?

THE BOY begins to paint black power line images of his animals. THE OLD MAN watches the boy paint.

THE OLD MAN

I wanted to paint on the scrolls. I wanted to paint on as many scrolls as I could. They said I was too young … That it wasn't right … that I was a threat to the society. That it was taboo. They said I was too young to keep company with the elders. "You should spend time with boys your own age."

THE BOY

I don't want to. I want to paint.

THE OLD MAN

Then paint. Good boy. Stupid but good. Paint.

THE BOY looks through the opening of the tent.

THE BOY

Can I come in the tent with you?

THE OLD MAN

Can you come in the tent with me? I just want to sleep … by myself peace.

THE BOY

It's lonely out here.

THE OLD MAN

It's lonely in here too.

THE BOY climbs up on the bed and takes THE OLD MAN's hand like a grandson to a grandfather.

THE BOY

You don't have to worry, I won't leave you.

THE OLD MAN

What if I leave you?

THE BOY

At home nobody was alone. We all lived in one room.

THE OLD MAN

At home nobody was alone. We all lived in one room.

THE OLD MAN / THE BOY

We all slept in one room.

THE OLD MAN

We all dreamed in one room and listened to the stories and listened to each other's hearts. We were at one.

THE OLD MAN / THE BOY

We were at once one.

THE OLD MAN

For an eternity.

THE BOY stands tall on the bed. Reaching up he points his finger and a black line continues and begins to draw the outline of a white bear, a turtle, a bird etc. THE OLD MAN stands and does the same and like two young boys they bring the tent to life with the images of their spirit, mind and imagination.

As they draw the sound of each animal becomes clear in the tent and mixes with each other. The drawing gets faster and faster, the noise gets louder and louder.

THE BOY and THE OLD MAN carry on loudly in a room of their making.

A door tunnel opens and so does the faraway image of a woman's body and the sound of her heels clicking from afar and drawing closer. Her flashlight penetrates the water and tent.

And finally we see her in 1950s splendor. She wears a wet housedress, a bathing cap, and cat glasses. She is the ultimate Auntie who ruins everybody's lives.

AUNTIE (*loudly*)

What's going on in there? I said, What's going on in there?

Silence.

Yes ... well ... You think I don't know what's going on in there. Just because I'm white and asking, doesn't mean I don't know what's going on in there.

Silence.

I see everything ... You hear me?

THE OLD MAN (*whispers in conspiracy to THE BOY*)

Nothing ... Don't say nothing ... she's a bitch of an Aunt ... once a bitch always a bitch ... don't say nothin' ...

AUNTIE

I'm not stupid ... I can see what's going on in there. You don't have to have 20/20 vision to see everything. Even if I have to wear glasses because, God knows, it's hard seeing everything. I can still see savages.

She listens. Silence.

I can see what you are up to ... which is no good. You should go to school that's what you should do. Get a trade. You should go to school and learn something useful instead of drawing those stupid pictures.

THE OLD MAN

I went to school. I got your grade four and then some for all the good it did me.

He talks to THE BOY.

THE OLD MAN

You gotta learn your own education.

AUNTIE

What did you say?

THE BOY

Nothin'.

THE OLD MAN

Nothin'. The boy said nothin'.

AUNTIE

You should go to residential school and learn how to smile. Never underestimate the power of being useful and learning how to smile. The right smile can get you through a lot of doors especially if you are a useful Indian.

THE OLD MAN

Don't listen to her squeaking ...

THE BOY slowly continues the drawing line.

AUNTIE

Stop that useless pagan scratching when I'm talking. That boy is rude and useless. Bullheaded! Try to give an Indian advice and see what where it gets you. Nowhere. What do I care?

THE OLD MAN

You have to decide your own future ... What are you going to do?

AUNTIE

What are you going to do with your life? One of these days ... you're going to learn ...

THE BOY / THE OLD MAN

/I'm going to ... He's going to ...

AUNTIE

... learn his lesson. One of these days he is going to learn his lesson and I'm going to be there. I'm going to ...

THE BOY (*this could be spoken in Ojibway*)

I'm going to be a Shaman!

AUNTIE

Yes! What did you say? I can't understand that devil speak ...

THE OLD MAN

He said he's going to be a Shaman. Deal with it ...

AUNTIE

Useless! Useless! Bullheaded Indian!

THE BOY

I am going to school ...

AUNTIE

I think he said he's going to school ...

THE OLD MAN

You just hear what you like ...

AUNTIE

Yes! By God ... he's going to school ... he's seen the light! Powerful ... Powerful ... Lord ... Amen!

THE OLD MAN

And then ... He's going to leave school ... What do you think of that!

AUNTIE

Useless ... useless ... unsmiling bullheaded Indians ...

THE OLD MAN smiles, satisfied.

THE OLD MAN

Well ... geez ... you gotta have a personal belief.

AUNTIE

Mark my words you're going to learn your lesson ...

THE OLD MAN

No! He's gonna live his own life ...

AUNTIE

You're going to learn the lesson of your life. Which is ... nobody gets to live their own life ... and I'm gonna be here to say "I told you so." ... Yessirree, mark my words ... you're gonna wish you listened to your old Auntie ... Nobody lives their own life on this planet ... You hear me ...

Complete quiet. AUNTIE, frustrated by the silence, hesitates and then clicks her flashlight out. The sound of her footsteps echoes down a long hallway.

THE OLD MAN listens to her heels click down the long hallway.

THE OLD MAN

That woman messed up my whole life.

THE BOY takes his hand and THE OLD MAN tosses it away softly ...

THE OLD MAN

Give me some space now. Roll up those scrolls if you wanna be "useful."

THE OLD MAN sits down and sulks over the memory.

THE BOY begins to slowly curl up his canvasses into scrolls.

SANDY LAKE, 1962

As he stands with an armful of scrolls, a long tunnel of a doorway lights up and a man's image appears from afar.

The sound of his footsteps approaches.

THE BOY looks at THE OLD MAN

THE OLD MAN

What now?

THE BOY

Someone's coming …

THE OLD MAN

Then go see.

THE BOY

No, you go see …

THE OLD MAN slowly rises …

THE OLD MAN

What's the point of being an old man, if you're the one who has to do everything …

THE BOY approaches him and pulls at his arm …

THE OLD MAN

I can do it … I can get up … get the scrolls … Hold onto them now …

THE BOY gathers the scrolls but drops them … THE BOY frantically tries to pick them up.

THE BOY looks up to see the black shoes and white suit of JACK—a smartly-dressed art agent who smiles down at THE BOY, trying to set him at ease.

JACK

I hear you are a great painter. I heard there was a great painter in the woods.

THE BOY looks at THE OLD MAN.

THE OLD MAN

I have been painting everything I see since I can remember.

JACK

Is that right?

THE OLD MAN

That's right Jack ... that's right ... It feels good to say it.

THE OLD MAN looks at THE BOY.

JACK

My name is Jack ... I'm an art agent ... I was just travelling through and your name was mentioned to me by a number of people ... You are Norval Morrisseau, yes?

THE OLD MAN

Don't just stand there staring like a boy ... grow up ... say something smart ... Jesus ... he's going to think you're an idiot ...

THE BOY slowly rises and opens his mouth, but nothing comes out.

JACK

Cat got your tongue?

THE OLD MAN

Probably ... Misshipeshu, give the boy his tongue back! This is serious business here ...

THE OLD MAN reaches down and fumbles around in the darkness under the bed. There is the sound of things being fumbled around with—THE OLD MAN grabs the tail of a Norval white cat—he raises it and it screeches protest. THE OLD MAN grabs a small Norval dog's tail and raises it and it barks out in fear, he grabs a Norval serpent by the tail and it hisses fearfully.

His hand finally fishes around dramatically and grabs the leg of a tall man. THE OLD MAN pulls mightily and the body of the tall handsome YOUNG MAN emerges wet and spread out on the floor at the feet of JACK. THE YOUNG MAN looks up slowly, shoes to white impeccable pants, to suit jacket, into the handsome face of JACK, smiling down.

THE OLD MAN

The first time I saw him he seemed so tall he couldn't possibly fit through any door. We stood like two equals … like an Indian meeting John Wayne. Like a fish out of water meeting a white suit.

JACK

I said, I heard there was a great painter in the woods and it seemed like quite the mystery … so I was curious … I'm sorry … I probably caught you at an inconvenient time …

THE OLD MAN

Get up for christsakes … Say something for yourself.

THE YOUNG MAN rises uncomfortably, trying to ride down his wet clothes and look normal. JACK looks around at his work on every surface.

JACK

I'm Jack, like I said and you must be …

He holds out his hand knowingly.

THE YOUNG MAN

I'm Norval Morrisseau. My Indian name is Copper Thunderbird. I have been painting everything I see since I can remember.

JACK

I believe you.

THE OLD MAN

Say something smart.

THE YOUNG MAN

I'm Ojibway …

THE OLD MAN

Jesus …

JACK

I'm from Toronto.

THE OLD MAN

I don't know who's worse.

JACK

Can I see your paintings? … The ones you have in your hands …

THE BOY motions "No" … but both THE OLD MAN and THE YOUNG MAN give him the look. THE BOY begins to spread them out on the floor and then falls behind the tall legs of THE YOUNG MAN sneaking a peak.

THE YOUNG MAN

I watched him look at my paintings as they rolled out. Watched for anything in his body that gave way to his eyes and then his words. I watched his body look at my paintings. Watched when he moved, when he breathed in this way, or that.

JACK unrolls another one and looks into it.

THE OLD MAN

I waited for him to look up and hoped the white suit from the city would not patronize me. That his big city head wouldn't say "how adorable," or "isn't it 'nice' that someone was documenting the primitive images of a long gone people."

JACK slowly stands up and looks at THE YOUNG MAN. They stand as equals.

THE YOUNG MAN

When he looked up. When he unbended his body from my scrolls. He was tall. Almost as tall as an Indian.

THE YOUNG MAN looks at him intently.

THE YOUNG MAN

Are you part Indian?

THE OLD MAN

You can tell us Jack ...

JACK

No.

THE OLD MAN

Liar.

JACK

My grandmother was Indian but she kept it a secret.

THE YOUNG MAN

Why?

JACK

Because she didn't know what else to do ... I guess.

JACK squirms for the first time, embarrassed.

THE YOUNG MAN

That's a good answer.

THE OLD MAN

That's a closet Indian. And there be a lot of closets ...

THE BOY (*this could be spoken in Ojibway*)

What do you think of my scrolls/?

THE YOUNG MAN

What I meant to say is ... What do you think of my paintings?

All THREE NORVALS stop in suspense. Silence.

JACK

I think you're a good artist and your work deserves to be known.

THE OLD MAN begins to do a victory dance. THE YOUNG MAN and THE OLD MAN stand shoulder to shoulder looking at each other.

THE YOUNG MAN

I think I'm looking at an Indian in a white suit.

THE OLD MAN

Just kiss him why don't you and get it over with ... Geez ...

THE OLD MAN waves them away and moves toward his bed. THE BOY follows THE OLD MAN, watching everything.

JACK and THE YOUNG MAN begin to walk together, all the while looking down at the images on the scrolls.

JACK

I want to exhibit your work in my gallery in Toronto, is that something you'd be interested in?

THE YOUNG MAN

I have been waiting for this moment for a long time and I am ready.

JACK

Do you mind if I ask you a question?

THE YOUNG MAN

Ask if you want to ...

JACK

These symbols here ... on every painting ... what do they mean?

THE YOUNG MAN

They mean I have been marked by the power of the Thunderbird, and by love.

JACK

Explain it to me.

THE YOUNG MAN

It's a long story ...

JACK

I have all the time in the world.

THE YOUNG MAN smiles.

THE YOUNG MAN

How Indian did you say you were? ... Hmm ... See for yourself then ...

THE YOUNG MAN reaches the doorway tunnel of JACK's. They shake hands. THE YOUNG MAN gives him the scrolls and JACK walks to his desk and sits down to watch the story unfold ...

SANDY LAKE RESERVE, 1950

The sound of a 1950s heap of garbage drops down on THE YOUNG MAN ...

THE YOUNG MAN

Shit ...

THE YOUNG MAN steps on things in disgust and then begins to buckle over in pain holding his chest, he crawls to the top of the heap on all fours.

THE OLD MAN

I don't care what they say ... it's not easy to die ... It takes a lot of focus.

THE YOUNG MAN

I don't feel so well.

THE BOY

He doesn't look so good.

THE YOUNG MAN begins to puke noisily.

THE OLD MAN

It's the sound of love.

THE BOY

Love?

THE OLD MAN

Somebody's love gone bad right inside your belly. It reminds me of this real beautiful Indian woman I used to know ... Real sweet ... a pretty thing that turned ugly. You see she loved me ... but I didn't love her back. That can undo a man.

THE YOUNG MAN

Can somebody help me out here?

Three shadowy forms on all fours emerge from behind him like large DUMP BEARS. They look through the garbage, eating leftovers and reading scraps of magazines ... sniffing and trying on old clothes ...

DUMP BEAR TWO

You probably just got indigestion. That means it's something you ate.

DUMP BEAR THREE

Or something you drank.

THE YOUNG MAN

My head is startin' to hurt ...

DUMP BEAR THREE

It's probably just all in your mind ... 'cause a lot of problems spring from the mind. I read that. Wait a minute, the article is here somewhere ...

THE YOUNG MAN begins to stagger.

THE YOUNG MAN

The thing is I don't feel so good ...

Rummages through the garbage.

THE OLD MAN

The thing is I was having this real nice courtship with this medicine woman's daughter ... Real nice ... and then all of a sudden she has to ruin everything by telling me she loved me ... And when she asked me if I loved her I said ...

A wave of nausea hits THE YOUNG MAN ... he bends over to retch ...

THE YOUNG MAN

"No ... God ... no ...

DUMP BEAR TWO

Dumb. You should say yes even and especially if you mean no. I've been keeping up with those Dear Abby women letter writers and even if women say they want the truth, you can be damn sure they don't want *your* truth.

THE OLD MAN

Anyways, so I tell her I don't love her ... everything is fine for a minute. She gives me a nice tea like a real trustworthy woman. I drink it and then look down into the cup and all sorts of leaves and herbs look back at me. Never a good sign. No future in that tea cup.

DUMP BEAR THREE

Nope. You'd been poisoned.

THE OLD MAN

The oldest trick in the book.

THE YOUNG MAN

Hey ... there's blood comin' from my nose ... See ...

THE YOUNG MAN stands in disbelief, touching his nose and wiping the blood from it as it streams down.

DUMP BEAR ONE

You look like shit ...

THE OLD MAN

A spell had been cast down upon me by a powerful, powerful medicine woman, whose daughter I don't love ... So in desperation I go see a white doctor.

THE YOUNG MAN

Listen you fuckin' assholes ... I got this deep pain. I'm gonna die ... die ... die ...

THE YOUNG MAN digs in the dump and pulls out a bottle of prescription pills.

THE OLD MAN

Anyways, the white doctor just gives me some little pills ...

THE YOUNG MAN shakes them like a rattle and then opens the bottle.

DUMP BEAR ONE

Valium?

THE YOUNG MAN shoves the pills in his mouth.

THE YOUNG MAN

I love you … man …

THE OLD MAN

Valium? Who knows?

THE YOUNG MAN

Who cares …

DUMP BEAR TWO

They're over-prescribing, those doctors … just thank God you're not a housewife. On the other hand, Valium makes everybody Indian.

THE OLD MAN

Anyways, like I was trying to say, I take these pills … Nothing … I get sicker and sicker.

DUMP BEAR THREE

Let me guess … weaker and weaker.

THE OLD MAN

I'm just about to die.

THE YOUNG MAN lays down and covers himself with debris … and corpses …

THE YOUNG MAN

Fuck you guys … I'm dead.

THE DUMP BEARS

Let it be said he's just about to die.

THE YOUNG MAN

I'm dead already …

THE OLD MAN

It's not easy to die. But I say … I'm just about to die.

THE YOUNG MAN continues to cover himself with debris …

THE YOUNG MAN

Dead … Dead … Dead …

THE DUMP BEARS

Amen.

Hallelujah.

THE OLD MAN

Except my mother got me a more powerful medicine woman …

THE YOUNG MAN rises slightly with hope …

THE YOUNG MAN

Yeeeah?

THE OLD MAN

And she did something special. Real special …

The DUMP BEARS look down on THE YOUNG MAN.

THE YOUNG MAN

Yeah? Go on …

THE OLD MAN

She performed a sucking ritual on me.

The DUMP BEARS grunt. THE YOUNG MAN touches his penis.

THE YOUNG MAN

Now?/

DUMP BEAR ONE

/Now we're talking.

DUMP BEAR TWO

Not a good day to die.

THE OLD MAN

She sucks out the objects, or medicine that was lodged in my insides to get to a good feeling. She waits but nothing good is happening … so in desperation … she does the last thing she can do … She gives me the highest sort of power a medicine woman can give when everything looks hopeless. A last rite of sorts … She gives me a new name. A powerful new name that cures me …

THE DUMP BEARS

It is …

THE YOUNG MAN

I am.

The sound of thunder as THE YOUNG MAN looks up and rain begins to baptize him …

THE OLD MAN

Copper Thunderbird.

THE YOUNG MAN

And it is a new beginning.

THE YOUNG MAN backs onto the wall behind him and, as he does, lights flash in and out of the room. THE YOUNG MAN's body shines out as a copper petroglyph of a Thunderbird.

Below him THE OLD MAN's body appears spread out like an offering on the bed, his feet touching the standing feet of THE YOUNG MAN. They look at each like the two sides of reflection in water.

The thunder increases as does the sound of the rain, leaving droplets of sweat marks on the back wall like clouds and raindrops.

The thunder and clouds begin to move and to separate THE OLD MAN and THE YOUNG MAN.

THE BOY climbs closer to the Copper Thunderbird petroglyph and THE YOUNG MAN inside it. He begins to draw a new line—his own out of the story unfolding. He draws the outline of THE YOUNG MAN Norval. He draws the Thunderbird Headdress throughout …

THE BOY sings under in Ojibway.

THE OLD MAN

Aahh. We believed, the Ojibway believe, the thunder is a great massive bird called Thunderbird whose eyes shoot out lightning and thunder. The first thunder in early spring is something good to hear …

THE YOUNG MAN watches THE BOY as he continues to outline him into the vision story.

Norval THE YOUNG MAN in Thunderbird, appears from above the clouds …

THE OLD MAN

The Ojibway welcome home their protector again from its home in the south where it has been all winter. Offerings of tobacco were placed on the ground, or the water. It is known that the Thunderbirds have a huge nest on mountains of the Earth, and large blankets of clouds always cover the nest although the Thunderbird is never seen to come and go from its nest … it was always known to be there.

THE YOUNG MAN

I am going to breathe these stories into the world. I am going to draw them the way I feel them. The way I see them and like a Thunderbird, like the Copper Thunderbird that is me, this new power will allow me to draw the lines, the power lines, that will leave the stories of my people on the world so that they too can not only see them, but feel them, be a part of them, a part of the knowing that we, the Ojibway will always be here.

The DUMP BEARS advance all carrying beers in their paws. DUMP BEAR ONE pushes THE YOUNG MAN out of the image.

DUMP BEAR ONE

What did you say?

THE YOUNG MAN

I said ... this new name has given me the power to draw what I am supposed to draw.

DUMP BEAR TWO

I'm sure the elders have something to say about that.

THE YOUNG MAN

What do you have to say?

DUMP BEAR ONE

I say, you're full of shit. But that's alright, look where we're sitting ... Don't be pissed off ... I know you got this big name and everything but what good is it ... I say, that like the rest of us, your dreams will end up here just like ours have ... in a garbage dump. In a white man's garbage dump.

DUMP BEAR TWO

What do you think someone's going to discover you ... rescue you in this shit hole?

He picks up a dirty Playboy *magazine from the dump heap.*

DUMP BEAR THREE

Anyways, you gotta have big tits to be rescued.

DUMP BEAR TWO

Good one.

THE DUMP BEARS

Or at least be white.

DUMP BEAR ONE

Okay ... You ever read about an Indian being rescued. Look at you ... you have read almost every fuckin' thing in this dump, for what years, and let me guess ... you probably haven't read one story about an Indian being rescued.

DUMP BEAR TWO

Case in point, Perry Mason/

DUMP BEAR ONE

/Shut up.

DUMP BEAR THREE

... Discovered and killed maybe. But never rescued.

DUMP BEAR ONE

We are invisible. We don't exist. Nobody can see us. And if you were to die tomorrow there would be nobody but us that gave a shit ... So cheer up.

THE OLD MAN

Why die tomorrow when you can die today ...

DUMP BEAR ONE extends a beer to THE YOUNG MAN's hand. The DUMP BEARS raise their beers in a cheer. They cheer louder as THE YOUNG MAN seems to accept the beer but then extends his arms in the air like a Thunderbird ... /

/The sound of mechanical thunder and lightning flashes light and then dark revealing the DUMP BEARS and THE YOUNG MAN frozen in their positions. Time elongates.

THE YOUNG MAN begins to to cough deeper and deeper.

FORT WILLIAM SANITARIUM, 1956

The sound transforms again and lights flash revealing a giant x-ray machine that takes a picture and leaves the x-ray positive image of THE YOUNG MAN's skeleton.

Again, but far off, the sound of a giant x-ray machine takes a picture and this time leaves the x-ray positive image of a woman's skeleton.

THE YOUNG MAN walks out from behind his skeleton wearing a dark blue hospital gown. HARRIET walks out from behind her skeleton wearing a light blue hospital gown. From across the space they look down at themselves. At their skeletons.

They look at each other's bones. They look at each other.

HARRIET smiles.

HARRIET

I see you.

HARRIET turns to leave and THE YOUNG MAN follows. He follows her and then feels something behind him. HARRIET feels him stop and turns to watch throughout. THE YOUNG MAN turns into the woodlands. It is green and lush but suddenly a gigantic Norval Sacred Bear looms over him.

THE YOUNG MAN

What now bear? What's coming now ... ?

He panics and moves away from it and as he does he backs into a river and Norval lynx-like serpents appear squirming towards him, chewing bones and fuming. He begins to sweat with the terrible fever of death.

THE YOUNG MAN

I have a fever that's all it is. A terrible fever coming from my chest. I am seeing things this way ... snakes again ... and that ... green woods ... seeing things a man sees when he's in between life and death.

He stands in incredible fear between worlds and demi-gods.

THE BOY appears behind THE YOUNG MAN and whispers to him.

THE BOY

We have to run from this death ...

THE OLD MAN appears behind them and whispers to them.

THE OLD MAN

I never heard of anyone outrunning TB ...

THE YOUNG MAN

What choice do I have?

THE YOUNG MAN begins to run, THE BOY begins to run, THE OLD MAN begins to run. Their breathing heaving in exertion.

THE YOUNG MAN

Dear Manitou, help me! Help me, I'm dying ...

THE BOY

Holy Mother of God pray for us sinners now and at the hour of our death ... I mean Manitou ...

THE YOUNG MAN

I mean Jesus Manitou ...

THE OLD MAN stops, and stops them ...

THE OLD MAN

I mean ... fuck me I'm old ... I can't run away anymore!

The sound of a giant white buffalo begins to thunder behind them. They look past the sound …

THE OLD MAN

If we can't run from it … we will run with it … Free and fearless we will run like the buffalo across a great prairie.

Twenty feet tall, the white buffalo towers over them, and as it passes above them, they follow.

As they run the sky opens and stars begin to shine, and a yellow field emerges brilliantly. The sound of their feet and breath pound into the ground as one.

The white buffalo finally runs past them and THE YOUNG MAN falls down with THE BOY breathless. THE THREE NORVALS try to catch their breath.

The space turns night dark blue and then bright, light sky blue. They look up and whisper to each other …

THE OLD MAN

Did you see the serpents?

THE YOUNG MAN

Yes …

THE OLD MAN

Were you afraid of them?

THE YOUNG MAN

Yes.

THE BOY

Did you see the bear?

THE YOUNG MAN

Yes.

THE BOY

Were you afraid of him?

THE YOUNG MAN

Yes.

THE OLD MAN

Are you afraid of the Thunderbird?

THE YOUNG MAN looks at THE BOY.

THE YOUNG MAN / THE BOY

Not much.

They all begin to laugh …

THE OLD MAN

All these things that we were afraid of are now down ... destroyed ... vanished! We were just being tested. Tested to see how afraid our fear was ... From now on these blues are going to protect us.

The bodies of THE YOUNG MAN, THE BOY and THE OLD MAN turn light blue ... and then dark blue.

THE OLD MAN

Two blues. One dark, like this night blue, and the other light, like this day next. Two blues that will go back and forth to protect us from all things of the demi-gods. All things of their black and white sorcery. We should paint between the blues. Between the lines of days and nights. Paint between worlds, between us without fear.

The dark blue night fades into light blue over and over again. THE OLD MAN and THE BOY saturate into the blue and disappear.

There is nothing but THE YOUNG MAN in blue until two beautiful brown arms reach around him and hold him embracing the blue.

HARRIET (*from behind*)

I have loved you from the beginning.

THE YOUNG MAN

Ahhhhh ... Who's there?

HARRIET (*whispering*)

Who were you expecting?

THE YOUNG MAN

It can get complicated.

HARRIET

Then make it simple.

She wraps her arms around him deeply, she kisses him softly, she moves her face close to his seductively.

THE YOUNG MAN

Harriet ... I would know your arms anywhere ... I would know your lips anywhere ... I would know the smell of your skin anywhere ... but tell me again what vision is this ...

HARRIET

A vision who has loved you from the beginning.

He turns toward her. They kiss.

HARRIET raises her legs and arms around THE YOUNG MAN like a frog. He holds her leg up as she kisses him passionately.

HARRIET

I have loved you hard from the beginning of you and I. I have loved you deeply. Hold me now tightly. Hold me, hold me deep inside.

THE YOUNG MAN

How tight can I hold you against my own self? How long can we hold ourselves against ourselves?

HARRIET (*this could be spoken in Cree*)

I love you … I love you Norval. We belong to each other.

HARRIET undresses THE YOUNG MAN. Taking off his shirt she whispers seductively in his ear, and begins to paint his name in Cree on his chest and, as she does, the symbols appear large behind them in red ochre. He breathes heavily and pulls her face into his.

A knock on the door.

They freeze.

AUNTIE THE NURSE

Norval!

Lights up on the ultimate AUNTIE dressed as a nurse. HARRIET and THE YOUNG MAN pull the sheet across their bodies and over their heads.

AUNTIE THE NURSE

No use playing dead … I know you're in there and I know what's going on in there … Just because I'm not there doesn't mean I can't see what's going on between a young man and a young woman. I was a young person once too you know? I know young people of your age have certain urges. But it's best just to suppress them. Nobody ever made themselves eternally happy giving in to an urge. Now I understand almost dying has a way of making you/

THE OLD MAN

/Wanna fuck …

AUNTIE THE NURSE

Pardon me/

THE YOUNG MAN

/Wanna duck ...

AUNTIE THE NURSE

Right! Ummm ... Now let's all go back to our respective rooms shall we ...

Silence.

THE OLD MAN makes the sound of a bullfrog.

AUNTIE THE NURSE

Bullheaded frogs! You know you two should be resting and not getting yourselves excited when you can't breathe. You'll only have yourselves to blame for carrying on ...

AUNTIE THE NURSE waits for a response. There is none.

Bullheaded frogs! I'm going now. Bye. Bye. Good riddance ... here I go ...

AUNTIE THE NURSE walks down a long hallway. Her footsteps echo down. She tiptoes back. They come out from under the sheet.

THE YOUNG MAN

I had a vision.

HARRIET

I was having a vision. Then a nightmare, and now ...

He kisses her.

HARRIET

I'll tell you mine if you tell me yours first ...

THE YOUNG MAN

I'll show you mine if you show me yours first ...

HARRIET

That's not how it works.

THE YOUNG MAN

Why?

HARRIET

Because you're the visionary.

THE YOUNG MAN

How do you know?

HARRIET

Because I see it in you.

He walks away.

THE YOUNG MAN

You can see it in me. Really? … because I really feel it in me now. It's hard to explain but I feel like everything has changed inside me.That maybe all this dying has killed my fear, and being saved each time has made me stronger. Made me the Thunderbird, made me take that line and fill it with colour so that I can save myself. To paint what I have to to paint without fear. To let the stories come from me, through me, with the power and the colour of our bones with no apology … Finally no apologies. I will not fear anything, or anyone.

HARRIET

And what do your higher eyes see here?

THE YOUNG MAN

That I should not be afraid to love.

He takes his hand and begins to draw on her naked body. She reacts to his touch as he paints their house and seven children in red ochre on her skin. Throughout the following it is displayed larger behind them, including them in the love vision.

HARRIET

I had a vision I was your wife …

THE YOUNG MAN

… I was your husband …

HARRIET

And we lived in the woods … and you painted …

THE YOUNG MAN

… and I looked after you.

HARRIET

… and we made love … and had seven babies … and we lived together …

THE YOUNG MAN

Forever stuck together with this …

HARRIET

… With this love.

They make love noisily.

THE OLD MAN sticks his fingers in his ears to stop the increasing noise and looks at them, agitated.

THE OLD MAN

Jesus ...

A loud knock on the door.

AUNTIE THE NURSE

I hear you ... bullheaded intercoursing frogs!

The sound of an underwater dog barking, and barking in the distance.

THE OLD MAN

Now the dogs ... fuckin' dogs.

AUNTIE THE NURSE looks at her watch impatiently. Lights go down on her as she walks down a long hallway, the sound of her footsteps echoing away. The sound of barking gets closer and closer.

The sound of love making gets louder and louder. The sound of barking gets closer and closer. The sound of lovemaking gets louder.

THE OLD MAN

Shut up over there ... a woman is a woman but how long does this have to go on?

The two lovers ignore him. The bed creaks and creaks.

RED LAKE, 1959

A strange-looking man appears in the doorway of a tunnel. He is an exaggerated European, with a big nose, glasses and an accent. He wears a long dark cloak that floats behind him and speaks in garbled underwater English.

He walks toward the room. He can't see very well.

Lights up and down as THE BOY draws the outline of a Norval dog and a Norval horned cat. The dog watches the outline of the cat become real and then rushes to chase it barking after it down a long shadow tunnel. It echoes.

DR. WEINSTEIN

Now don't go down there … puppy … puppy? Come back my little viener schnitzel … my little sauerkraut …

THE OLD MAN

Too bad about the puppy.

DR. WEINSTEIN

Who said that?

Silence.

I can hardly hear you. What did you say?

THE OLD MAN

I said, you fuck with the cat you lose a dog.

DR. WEINSTEIN

Pardon me?

THE OLD MAN

I said you eat a bear you get the shits.

DR. WEINSTEIN

(*uncomfortable*) I see.

THE OLD MAN

I don't think you do. You think you do, but you don't.

DR. WEINSTEIN

Right … um … Is the young man in? I was just taking my dog for a walk and thought I would drop in and give him some good news … There is an art agent coming from Toronto … and I am hoping they can connect …

THE OLD MAN just looks at him …

DR. WEINSTEIN

This is the chance he has been waiting for … Could I just have a word with him briefly? Please …

THE OLD MAN

He's busy …

DR. WEINSTEIN

Are you his grandfather?

THE OLD MAN

No, I'm just an old man.

There is an uncomfortable silence.

DR. WEINSTEIN

I see … do you want a smoke?

THE OLD MAN elegantly takes the cigarette from the DOCTOR's hand. THE OLD MAN signals that THE YOUNG MAN is over there making love.

THE OLD MAN
I've been trying to quit but my nerves are bad …

DR. WEINSTEIN
My name is Doctor/

THE OLD MAN
/Maymaygwaysiwuk—Though I am mixing my metaphors. With the nose you got and the cloak from faraway, you looked like a maymaygwaysiwuk.

DR. WEINSTEIN
What's that?

THE OLD MAN
A mer-man. A mer-man offering something …

DR. WEINSTEIN
Well, I have a little flask here of brandy … would you like a sip?

THE OLD MAN
You are in my living room and I will do the offering … Can I get you a beer?

THE OLD MAN rummages under his chair for a beer. He puts on a cigarette jacket and becomes quite cigarette jacket-ish.

DR. WEINSTEIN
European or domestic?

THE OLD MAN
Domestic and wild … you could say.

THE OLD MAN gives the beer to the doctor.

DR. WEINSTEIN
Alright, thank you … You can call me Dr. Weinstein.

THE OLD MAN
You can call me Dr. Morrisseau.

DR. WEINSTEIN smiles and begins to look around the space.

THE OLD MAN
We are both doctors of art. Are we not? Healers? What brings you to this neck of the woods?

DR. WEINSTEIN

Honestly, I was just curious where the young man lived. You see, as a rule he usually visits me and spends time in my library ... This is his home, really?

There is a long pause as THE YOUNG MAN has great sex.

THE YOUNG MAN

YES ... IT ... IS ... hmmmm.

There is a sex drift.

THE OLD MAN

Home is where the heart is. He means to say "Yes, he lives here" ... We all live here ... Us Indians that is ...

DR. WEINSTEIN

You see I met him in a chance meeting and have been encouraging him to paint ...

THE YOUNG MAN

They just moved from London, England—can you believe that? And they collect things ... antiques and art ... and/

THE OLD MAN

/Let me guess ... Indians ...

THE YOUNG MAN

No, they gave me some painting supplies ... and they have thousands of books on art. Can you believe that?

THE OLD MAN

(*to NORVAL THE YOUNG MAN*) Don't let him fuck you.

DR. WEINSTEIN

What did you say?

THE OLD MAN

I said ... I have quite the extensive library myself.

He points to his brain.

THE OLD MAN

Everything's up here ... A self-made man, you could say. A student of the universe. A ...

THE YOUNG MAN looks up from his lovemaking and responds.

THE YOUNG MAN

Listen, he's not into fucking young Indian boys ...

THE OLD MAN

I know ... It's just a blanket statement ... You usually can't trust a European that collects things ... especially if you're an Indian ...

THE YOUNG MAN

You're drinking ...

THE OLD MAN

So what.

A long pause. DR. WEINSTEIN looks at an open scroll.

DR. WEINSTEIN

Amazing ... just amazing ... With these drawings you can be a representative. "*The* representative." You can offer a look into the rich tunnels of the Ojibway mind and spirit. Your work could take you far ... even Paris ...

THE YOUNG MAN begins to disengage ...

THE YOUNG MAN

Do you really think so?

HARRIET pulls him back down on her.

THE OLD MAN

Do you really think it comes without a price? ... Stick to what you know ...

THE OLD MAN moves forward offensively.

THE OLD MAN

And you ... enough! ... Leave well enough alone. He doesn't know ... alright ... he doesn't know how much it will cost.

DR. WEINSTEIN

I do. I truly believe you could be The Father of Contemporary Indian Art!

There is silence. THE OLD MAN looks at DR. WEINSTEIN and hesitates, then begins to pace.

THE OLD MAN

Can an old man have a drink ... Can an old man sleep without being someone's father?

THE YOUNG MAN reaches under the bed with a free arm, pulls out a scroll and waves DR. WEINSTEIN over ...

THE YOUNG MAN

Here ... take this painting here then ... I have signed it for this occasion. Take it and in your travels to Europe, give it to Picasso.

DR. WEINSTEIN

Yes ... yes ... I/

Under his breath.

THE OLD MAN

/I could be the Father of Contemporary Indian Art?

THE YOUNG MAN

Thank you.

He looks at the lovers trying to make the decision again ...

THE OLD MAN

Shut up, shut up ... I'm trying to think ... shut up with all your squeaking ...

DR. WEINSTEIN backs away slowly. THE OLD MAN moves toward the bed. The two lovers ignore him.

DR. WEINSTEIN

... Alrighty then ... thank you ... uh ...

THE OLD MAN

/I said shut up ... SHUT up ... with this squeaking.

DR. WEINSTEIN

/I ... I ... I think I can let myself out ... thank you ...

THE OLD MAN

How long does it have to go on? I'm an old man for christsakes. I don't have as much stamina. I need to think. I need peace. I need myself. I need ... I need ... I need a piece of myself. Jesus look at them leap frog. This leap frog love is driving me crazy!

THE OLD MAN stumbles on the bed. He falls on the back of THE YOUNG MAN, squished between HARRIET and THE OLD MAN, THE YOUNG MAN struggles to get free.

THE YOUNG MAN

I can't breathe ... Harriet! I can't breathe.

HARRIET

I love you Norval.

THE YOUNG MAN

I love you ... I ...

THE OLD MAN whispers desperately into THE YOUNG MAN's ear.

THE OLD MAN

I am ... I am ... in love with you. I can give you everything you want. I will let you breathe and paint ... you will see everything ... you will touch everything ... you will fuck everything ... you will have money ... you will have famous ... You will love me for it. Fuck me and you will love me for it fucking you.

THE OLD MAN rolls THE YOUNG MAN over and toward himself. They began to kiss. HARRIET pulls away beginning to cry. She reaches to get back on frog-like to her man. There is a struggle between THE OLD MAN and HARRIET. THE OLD MAN raises his hand to strike her. She backs away crying.

THE OLD MAN then holds his hands out to HARRIET as she cries backing away.

THE OLD MAN

Harriet ... it is me ... (*He begins to cry softly.*)

HARRIET

I don't know you ... I don't know who you are ...

THE OLD MAN

I had a vision you were my wife ... and we lived in the woods ... and you painted me ... and I looked after you ... And we made love ... and had seven babies ... and we lived together forever stuck together with this love.

THE BOY reaches under the bed and pulls out three suits. They are black 1960s suits made of rubber. THE BOY reaches toward THE YOUNG MAN and they disrobe him and begin to try and put on his wet suit. They do the same for THE BOY. It is a suitable struggle, to stretch and tame the suit over their bodies. Helping each other, they find THE OLD MAN and bend him into his wet suit.

They tie each other's ties, they smooth each other's hair. They stand, three beautiful Indian men encased in suits.

POLLOCK GALLERY, TORONTO, 1962

The white gallery space opens to a chorus of gallery-goers. It is incredibly white. The gallery begins to fill with gallery patrons and art—white wine chatter.

THE BOY begins to draw pictures.

THE OLD MAN saunters in and looks at the patrons and is given the free wine freely.

Civilized music plays and distorts and leads THE GALLERY ROOM CHORUS and THE FLOODING ROOM CHORUS into a strange carnival dance that begins slowly and increases in velocity.

The sound of the lake begins to rise …

JACK gets up from his desk and moves toward THE YOUNG MAN, shakes his hand and then looks around at the space … THE YOUNG MAN stands paralyzed as he looks at all the gallery-goers.

JACK

Norval … Jesus you're going to give me an ulcer … You're late … I can't believe you would be late for your first exhibit … What took you so long?

THE YOUNG MAN

It was a long story … I thought you said you had all the time in the world.

JACK

I lied. The gallery is filling up/

THE YOUNG MAN

/I was trying to get here … There's a lot of things I had to deal with … plus I had to find something to wear.

JACK

Cute.

THE YOUNG MAN

You think?

JACK

No … Yes … I mean you look handsome. Nice suit.

THE YOUNG MAN

Thanks. I had to find someone to borrow it from, which is not an easy task on the res …

JACK

I'm sorry … I should of thought of that.

THE YOUNG MAN

It's okay … I look good. That's the main thing.

JACK

Everybody's waiting for you to say a few words … you can keep it short … Just speak from your heart … You're nervous?

THE YOUNG MAN

No. Yes … I'm not good at talking …

JACK

Just thank them for coming … You are fidgeting … Don't fidget.

THE YOUNG MAN

The suit's too tight. It's trying to hurt my private parts …

JACK

Just think about all the work you've done … Alright here we go … for God sakes don't pull on your crotch …

THE YOUNG MAN

Alright …

THE YOUNG MAN stands on an art podium and smiles and smiles and then, in a humble but knowing manner, begins to address his audience.

A slight hush and then polite applause.

A long silence.

THE YOUNG MAN

I am Norval Morrisseau having the Indian name of Copper Thunderbird. I am a born artist—some people are born artists and others are not, this is the same way with Indians.

THE GALLERY ROOM CHORUS

He speaks English quite well. Those people are sure coming along.

THE OLD MAN looks up and down at THE GALLERY ROOM CHORUS. They look at him with disgust. He whispers loudly back ...

THE OLD MAN

Some people are born stupid and some people are not, this is the same with Indians ... Ha ... ha ...

THE OLD MAN begins to drink increasingly as he tries to protect THE YOUNG MAN from THE GALLERY ROOM CHORUS and THE FLOODING ROOM CHORUS that drifts in, creating the contrasting elements of a forceful current.

THE FLOODING ROOM CHORUS

Look at his suit. It looks too small for him. An Indian shouldn't wear a suit, anyways. Trying to be a white man will only make him look more Indian.

THE OLD MAN

Be quiet you, I think he looks good. He talks the good talk. If you would just zip your mouths for a minute you might hear something good for a change.

THE YOUNG MAN

I have grown up with many stories and legends of my people and I have made paintings of these legends on great sheets of birchbark, loadstone these with tempered water, colours and some on plywood, but very few people have obtained these, as of the present time.

THE GALLERY ROOM CHORUS

I wonder if he's going to sing for us. I love it when they sing. It's so, so deep. Excuse me, could you drum and sing for us?

THE FLOODING ROOM CHORUS

How'd he learn to talk like that? Look at him smile. How'd he learn to smile like that? Probably residential school. He looks assimilated alright. Small.

THE OLD MAN

You remind me of the story. Some story about a crab, or was it a turtle? Anyways, there's always someone, or something trying to bring you down once you make it.

THE YOUNG MAN

I paint what is inside me from the beginning.

THE GALLERY ROOM CHORUS

I don't think he went to art school. Do you think he has an education of any kind?

THE FLOODING ROOM CHORUS

There he goes talking like a white man selling our secrets like a pair of moccasins. There he goes …

THE OLD MAN

Shut up … Just shut up! You even know how to make a pair of moccasins.

Silence.

That's what I thought … know-it-all assholes.

THE YOUNG MAN

These paintings are worthy to be exhibited in a gallery, if accepted. These paintings depict a legend or some other Ojibway belief …

THE GALLERY ROOM CHORUS

I think those Indians just have to move on from the past. They lost. They just have to accept that and try to be like everybody else …

THE YOUNG MAN

I said these paintings depict a legend, or some other Ojibway belief/

THE FLOODING ROOM CHORUS

/Being sold out. Traitor.

THE YOUNG MAN

Each one … is from my heart, my spirit/

THE FLOODING ROOM CHORUS

/Selling out.

THE GALLERY ROOM CHORUS

Doesn't he look like a little boy up there? … I almost feel sorry for him.

THE BOY continues to paint and paint … and the paintings begin to fill with colour.

THE YOUNG MAN

Each one is a part of me, a part of us and is as purely uncorrupted as possible for a modern day Indian/

THE FLOODING ROOM CHORUS

/Who has sold his people out.

THE OLD MAN

WHO IS BEING FUCKED BY EVERYONE!

THE YOUNG MAN begins to falter …

THE OLD MAN

You have to say to yourself what benefit will it be to my people? You have to ask yourself over and over and over and over and over and over and over again because they don't understand the benefit.

JACK approaches the podium and tries to rescue THE YOUNG MAN …

THE YOUNG MAN

I have to ask myself what benefit will my work be to my people.

JACK

Thank you Norval for your work and your words. It's been quite the day … So if there are any questions. We'd like to keep it to a few … thank you for your consideration …

THE GALLERY ROOM CHORUS clammers together excitedly.

THE GALLERY ROOM CHORUS

How does it feel? How do you feel? How does it feel to be an Indian?

THE BOY's paintings begin to be caged by frames.

THE YOUNG MAN

I really need to say this … so that you understand … I do not wish my work to be exploited in any commercial way but to be properly used as an art form …

THE GALLERY ROOM CHORUS

How does it feel to be primitive? Are you excited?

THE YOUNG MAN

Ahh? Am I excited and … primitive? No, … I … I was saying I want my work to be properly used as an art form in its proper place by generations of Ojibway people to see in the future. I want to …

THE GALLERY ROOM CHORUS

Bravo … Bravo …

THE YOUNG MAN

I want … these paintings to be seen by generations … As well as to be appreciated by all our white brothers.

THE FLOODING ROOM CHORUS

You sold your own people out. You sold us out for the white man.

The crowd claps and chats.

Sweating, THE YOUNG MAN tries to get off the podium. THE GALLERY ROOM CHORUS pushes him back on.

THE GALLERY ROOM CHORUS

Tell us a story, Norval. Look this way for us. You are a Chief, are you not? The Chief of a conquered people. Or, are you a Shaman? Can you drum? Can you draw one of your cute line drawings for us? Have you ever been to the city before? Have you ever seen so many people?

THE OLD MAN

Shut up ... shut up over there. Can't you see what you're doing to him. You're putting him up but talking him down. Shut up! Shut up! Shut your crooked mouths!

THE GALLERY ROOM CHORUS

What are you going to do with all your money from the paintings? How are you going to spend your money? How does an Indian spend money?

THE YOUNG MAN

Jack, I'm hungry. I feel dizzy. I think I really need to eat something ...

THE OLD MAN places a glass of red wine in his hand.

THE OLD MAN

If they're not going away ... Drown 'em out ...

The gallery wine glass clinks turn into a Chinese restaurant. A Chinese dragon floats by and its mouth opens nightmarishly.

THE YOUNG MAN

Jack ... did you see that snake ... ?

JACK

It's a dragon Norval ... A Chinese dragon in a Chinese restaurant. It happens all the time.

THE YOUNG MAN

Really ... I think it looks like a snake ...

THE GALLERY ROOM CHORUS and THE FLOODING ROOM CHORUS follow him and join in with the Chinese dragon roaring and Chinese restaurant plates clink and distorted Chinese music adds a layer.

THE OLD MAN begins to pour a bottle of wine down himself and the THE YOUNG MAN.

THE OLD MAN

Drown 'em out …

THE GALLERY ROOM CHORUS

Would you like to try some chicken balls?

THE FLOODING ROOM CHORUS

You think you can get away with this?

THE YOUNG MAN

Drown 'em out …

THE GALLERY ROOM CHORUS

How about a fortune cookie?

THE FLOODING ROOM CHORUS

Confucius say … You've made a big mistake …

THE YOUNG MAN

I've made a big mistake.

THE OLD MAN

I've made a big mistake … The white man does not deserve my paintings! They should be destroyed here and now to protect the mystical culture of my forefathers! Shut up … Shut up—

THE YOUNG MAN

Just stop please just stop. I want to go back to my cabin, my hotel. Jack, I want to take this suit off. Could somebody help me take this wet suit off? It's drowning me.

JACK stands up and tries to steady him but he is swept away by the CHORUSES.

The CHORUSES pass the drunken Indian around the room … THE OLD MAN staggers behind.

THE YOUNG MAN

Please give me a bit of room to breathe. I can't breathe here. You're standing too close, too close, the buildings are too close. Could you just help me down? Get me down.

THE OLD MAN

Give him room lady … I'll knock your kooky heads off.

THE GALLERY ROOM CHORUS back away and begin to take each painting off the walls of the room.

THE BOY tries to stop them and then finally sits down in tears and sings softly to console himself.

THE OLD MAN unsteadily tries to steady and guide THE YOUNG MAN past the staring CHORUS.

THE OLD MAN

I don't give a shit how they use chopsticks, what fork goes first, what spoon goes last. This is how we eat in the woods: like we're hungry. Like it's been a long winter and look, FOOD.

They both fall down and finally sit and drink together, alone.

THE YOUNG MAN

It's been a long day hunting. I mean I bought an eight track cassette today. No? I never had one before. Thank you. It's been the longest day being in a circus. I mean being here and I just need to find silence for awhile like there is no tomorrow. It's like …

THE OLD MAN

Like I'm gonna drink this till there is no tomorrow … like there is no tomorrow. Like I don't care about their Barnum and Bailey Circus, or how much money they make, or their goddamn good intentions. I'm gonna tell them to get that chicken ball, or whatever it is, away from me. I don't know what goddamn sweet and sour is anyways!

THE GALLERY ROOM CHORUS take the last of his paintings and leave. THE YOUNG MAN suddenly rises abruptly.

THE YOUNG MAN

I want my paintings back! I shouldn't have brought them here. I shouldn't have let them look at them! I don't want their money. Take it back! I said take me back!

THE YOUNG MAN is left bare in the centre of the white space. He looks up and money begins to fall from the sky. He doesn't grab it, he just watches it fall around him. The money gradually rises up from his feet, submerging his legs and abdomen, his chest and finally his head throughout the following.

THE YOUNG MAN

The white man does not deserve my paintings ... the white man does not deserve my paintings ... take your money back ... I don't want money ... I don't deserve my paintings ... I'm gonna drink like there is no tomorrow ... I'm gonna drink like there is no tomorrow. Like there is no tomorrow, like there is no me ...

ACT 2

SANDY LAKE RESERVE, 1965

It is liquid blue.

THE THREE NORVALS float in the light blue and dark blue of the water. Their three black wet-suited bodies drift in contrast and in similarity through the blues of their water.

THE YOUNG MAN

Sometimes everything you are will drift your way under the caves where you sleep. Under yourself. Deep down where cats growl and serpents lie in great beds, and good things and bad things are said in the same water, where good things and bad things are said in the same sky, where good things and bad things are written in the same stone. Everything we are comes through the tunnels into the lake, into the river, into our blood streams. Rising the bones of a new story.

THE OLD MAN

There was a flood in me, a feeling that things submerged were rising to the surface and taking that surface over like a cleansing. Taking all my creatures two by two, in a white canoe through the caves of my mind. Reminding me that even though I am alone, so terribly alone. I am busy. I am busy with everything that I know, talking to me back and forth, like the dance of a lone boat on an empty sea.

THE BOY

You cannot judge the creatures that make you. You cannot say to yourself, you are ugly, you cannot be me. You have to include the beautiful and the sorrowful to look at, include them in the same water, the same earth, the same stone and know there is a bigger picture being written. A bigger knowing after the flood.

A white bone ladder comes down into the blue. THE YOUNG MAN *begins to climb with the help of* THE OLD MAN, THE OLD MAN *follows with a push from the* THE BOY. *Together they begin to climb the bone rungs.*

THE YOUNG MAN

I feel I have slowly climbed a ladder. Now I am at the top of that ladder. I can feel it sway, but I am not sure in what direction.

Two brilliant long white lights fade up as long train rails. The bright headlight of a train blares and the sound of the train engine draws closer to THE YOUNG MAN, THE OLD MAN *and* THE BOY *as they stand on the ladder, swaying from the motion-beast coming.*

THE YOUNG MAN

Jesus, is that you? I was thinking about the Bible really. Thinkin' about it the way I think about things—the Indian version.

The bright eye of the train gets brighter and brighter.

THE YOUNG MAN

Jesus, is that you, I said. No answer. You sure got bright eyes. A bright eye, one I guess, big. I see the light. I finally see the light.

THE OLD MAN

Why you have to see the light just before you die is beyond me. Why can't you see the light just to see it? Anyways, I'm more than ready.

THE YOUNG MAN *prepares himself to die with dignity. He spreads his arms out as he stands on the ladder.*

The eye of the train gets bigger and bigger until it is blinding as it whites out THE NORVALS. *The light and sound of it passes, leaving a vast darkness. In the dark,* THE YOUNG MAN *speaks alone.*

THE YOUNG MAN

It is dark. When it is dark. It is dark. The world in which we live is dark, and getting even darker.

THE YOUNG MAN lights a cigarette as he stands on the ladder and looks into the dark space. From the darkness—

HARRIET

Norval, can you get up and see to the children? Norval get up now ... don't just lay there like a man. Norval!

THE YOUNG MAN freezes confused.

THE YOUNG MAN

I'm not just lying here. I've been going places. Anyways, you're the woman, I'm the man. I'm lying down now as you say, and I'm having a vision. A vision. So you go and see to them. The crying.

HARRIET

I can't see to them either, Norval. Why? Because I'm having a vision I live in a house with a roof. You get up and let me lie here for a moment with this vision and let me think I live in a house with a roof, and a man that comes home every night. Oh, this vision is so good Norval, I wish you were here.

From the darkness a shadow shifts and THE OLD MAN is seen turning on a TV set from afar. The TV set blares on. It fills with static. The sound of static grows and the sound of crying children grows louder in the dark as Harriet calls to him.

THE YOUNG MAN looks over at the TV as HARRIET begins to shake THE YOUNG MAN's ladder.

HARRIET

Do you remember me, Norval? Norval? Can you hear me? Can you hear my voice? In my vision you come to me in the dark and lay down like you care. Remember me, Norval? Norval?

The static TV begins to blur as Norval's past wives come through the static embodied as full NORVAL WIVES.

THE THREE NORVAL WIVES

You are my husband. You are my husband. You are my husband.

HARRIET strikes a match and lights a candle.

HARRIET

You are my husband. Do you understand what that means? Stop looking at the TV set like something is going to happen. We have a TV but we don't have any heat. Maybe we should chop it up for kindling.

THE YOUNG MAN

I'm busy now. Can't you see I'm busy now?

HARRIET

Dreaming ...

THE YOUNG MAN

Remembering ...

HARRIET

Without me.

The THREE NORVAL WIVES caress THE OLD MAN lovingly and whisper in his ears, they position him in the middle of the square. They begin to dance for him like he is the only man in the world. THE YOUNG MAN climbs down from the ladder and begins to slowly walk toward them with desire.

THE YOUNG MAN

I want to feel free.

HARRIET

Without me.

The sound of a crying baby begins tagain. HARRIET gets up and moves in the dark, in the light of the candle. She picks up THE BOY from under the darkness and begins to comfort herself and the child by cooing. He cries again and again seven times over until she takes the burden to her chest and, crying softly, he soothes himself by suckling.

THE THREE NORVAL WIVES

In the same manner that you are enjoying us together, let you be loved by the women you desired to be loved by.

HARRIET

Norval ... please ...

Despite himself, THE YOUNG MAN walks toward THE THREE NORVAL WIVES.

THE YOUNG MAN

The crying. I should go back and soften the crying.

THE OLD MAN

Just tell her you are having a vision.

HARRIET stands up and moves toward him.

HARRIET

You don't have to tell her ... she has ears. She has heard it before, she has seen it all before. Norval, I swear it is the last vision without me.

THE THREE NORVAL WIVES

This is how she talks to you Norval. She doesn't understand what it is to be an artist. She doesn't understand the burden of being a visionary.

HARRIET

You have visions that are convenient for you and nobody else.

They open their mouths in a frog rebuttal.

THE THREE NORVAL WIVES

Why should you have to torment yourself over this one wife of yours? She's only a Cree woman, and a Cree woman is just like a pack dog! For you to be in this state over nothing!

THE YOUNG MAN

Harriet ... I ...

HARRIET touches his lips to silence him.

HARRIET

I am nothing. I am nothing but a woman crying in the dark for you, and you have left me nothing to leave. You have finally walked past our love.

Her fingers trail down to his chest where she traces the Cree letters of his name.

He takes her hand softly and then moves past her.

HARRIET picks up THE BOY and disappears into the darkness. The candle lights them down a long highway.

THE THREE NORVAL WIVES leave THE OLD MAN smugly. He grabs at them but they detach professionally.

THE YOUNG MAN looks to THE OLD MAN and touches his unmarked chest. It is quiet. They call across the space. THE OLD MAN drinks from a whiskey bottle. They begin to walk to the centre both ending up at a small round bar table and sitting in depression.

THE YOUNG MAN

Can you buy me a drink? I don't care what they say but when a woman leaves your room it always hurts your throat. I just feel so fuckin' thirsty you know what I mean. Parched. Like some kind of desert is coming.

THE OLD MAN

Tell me about it ... I don't feel so funny ... I feel like punching somebody ... I've made myself lonely.

THE BOY

I feel lonely too.

Lights up on THE BOY inside the Expo painting as a bear cub suckling the breast of a sensuous mother.

THE OLD MAN / THE YOUNG MAN

Shut up ...

THE YOUNG MAN

At least you have a tit to suck.

THE OLD MAN

And nobody's sucking on you.

THE YOUNG MAN

I got nothing to suck.

THE OLD MAN

Poor baby ...

THE YOUNG MAN

Shut up, I'm going through something here ...

THE OLD MAN

Whatever.

THE OLD MAN takes a drink of whiskey. THE YOUNG MAN motions for a swig but THE OLD MAN holds his own ...

THE YOUNG MAN

So where's all your good friends now?

THE OLD MAN

Dead, or drunk.

THE YOUNG MAN

What about your bear friends? Now that you're lonely they'll probably come and feel you up "just right" ... just like them three priests from residential school.

THE OLD MAN

Well ... once you been raped by priests there's no competition ... the first time is the deepest.

He begins to laugh at himself.

THE YOUNG MAN

... Seriously, if they knew you were here they would come and hump you like you were Goldilocks, or something.

THE OLD MAN

So ... what's it to you?

THE YOUNG MAN

I'm just telling you ... you should watch yourself better ... that's all ...

THE OLD MAN

Looks like you've been looking after yourself pretty good.

THE BOY

Nobody's listening to me.

THE YOUNG MAN / THE OLD MAN

Shut up ...

THE YOUNG MAN

What's that supposed to mean? I'm selling my wares, that's all ... it's a long tradition of Indian and art ... I'm trying to eat ...

THE OLD MAN

Fuck you ... You're a door to door salesman ... selling our art like a common fuckin' vacuum cleaner salesman ... you're a Hoover for booze ...

THE YOUNG MAN

At least I'm still painting ...

THE OLD MAN

You call that art?

THE YOUNG MAN

I call it "tourist art" ... It's not like I don't know the difference between "tourist" art and "fine" art ... when no one's buying, you gotta appeal to the masses ...

THE OLD MAN

That's beneath me ...

THE YOUNG MAN

How do you know what's beneath you when you're at the bottom?

THE OLD MAN staggers up slowly and menacingly, with balled up fists. THE YOUNG MAN gets up and cocks his fists.

THE OLD MAN

Fuck you ...

THE YOUNG MAN

No, fuck you ...

THE BOY

Can we stop fighting?

THE OLD MAN

Art is war!

THE YOUNG MAN

... And war makes me thirsty.

THE OLD MAN

Where's the paintings now?

THE YOUNG MAN

I'm sold out. Dry. I've been in every small town from here to Thunder Bay selling them.

THE OLD MAN

What about the big solo exhibits?

THE YOUNG MAN

Solitary. No sales.

THE OLD MAN

You call Jack?

THE YOUNG MAN

He sent some money, but I drank it. He sent some money and I drank it. He sent some money and I drank it ... you get the picture.

THE YOUNG MAN wanders over to THE BOY in the Expo painting all the time talking ...

THE YOUNG MAN

They ask me to paint them a mural for Expo in Montreal, so I say, "oui," and so it came ... but they didn't like it ... because the little bear cub ended up sucking the tit of a sensuous Earth. How am I to know what I am going to paint ... what is going to come? They asked me to modify my painting ... like you can modify an Indian. I told them to fuck themselves.

He touches THE BOY bear cub and the beautiful sensuous mother with his fingers as if he is painting them affectionately.

THE YOUNG MAN

You see ... you were getting nourishment from the earth and no white committee is going to understand the relationship between nourishment and mother, child and earth ... mother and woman ... all they see is sex ...

THE YOUNG MAN grabs THE BOY roughly from the painting and drags him over to the table. He grabs a stack of bar napkins and a pen and places them roughly in front of THE BOY.

THE YOUNG MAN

So fuck it ... fuck it ... fuck it ... let them leave my painting in the rain ... let them invite us in and leave us in the cold ... Draw!

THE OLD MAN

Leave the boy alone ... why don't you do your own tourist dirty work?

THE BOY begins to draw throughout. THE YOUNG MAN menacingly approaches THE OLD MAN.

THE YOUNG MAN

Why don't you give me a drink, old man?

THE OLD MAN takes a long sensuous drink of whiskey closing in on the end.

THE OLD MAN

I'm busy see ... drinking as I can and ... I'm rememberin' that time you got your first big time exhibit in Toronto ... a real surprise to the society ... and you came back with all this money.and you bought drinks for the whole town, for everyone one of us for weeks ...

THE OLD MAN laughs and finally passes the last of the whiskey to THE YOUNG MAN.

THE YOUNG MAN

... that was a good time then—wasn't it a good time—even if those two guys fell on the road and was runned over by that Smoky the Bear Forest Ranger. Not your fault they fell on their face. But it was a good time anyways.

THE OLD MAN

I always said you gotta keep your head up even if you fall on your face. I have always kept my head up. Even when I'm being run over I have done it. I have painted what I was supposed to paint.

THE YOUNG MAN

Now you give me the bottom of the bottle ... me, a part of your own blood ... I guess you gotten too famous for me now.

THE OLD MAN

A guy's got to look out for his own self.

THE YOUNG MAN

Yeah ... well ... I heard you been fuckin' men too/

THE OLD MAN

/What did you say?/

THE YOUNG MAN

/I wasn't gonna say anything but now that you gotten so uppity and cheap. You a cheap homosexual?

THE OLD MAN

I didn't fuck no man ... and what if I did? You gone all Christian on me now, eh? Now that I can't get you a drink you a big moral Christian now?

THE YOUNG MAN

Don't be looking at me ... I was never the Christian ... that's you and that boy's thinking ... What about another drink old man?

THE OLD MAN

I don't have any money for you. Get a job.

THE YOUNG MAN

You want maybe I should suck you off ... maybe that way you feel like a big Indian and can buy us a drink?

THE OLD MAN

Suck your own big Indian if it's long enough!

THE OLD MAN rips the napkins from THE BOY. He grabs THE YOUNG MAN by the shirt and stuffs the napkin drawings in his mouth ...

THE OLD MAN

Here … you're the salesman … hmmm? Go and sell them. Sell 'em cause I don't want to hear you talking anymore. Sell it and come back here and let's drink 'cause I'm tired of hearing your talk. You bore me with your needs, you make me want to puke. Sell it! Sell it! Let's drink!!!

THE OLD MAN shoves THE YOUNG MAN out.

THE OLD MAN

Whatta you looking at?

THE BOY

Nothing …

THE OLD MAN sits down in a pout. THE BOY kneels down on the bar floor.

THE BOY

Dear Jesus …

THE OLD MAN

He's not here … don't you know there's not a Jesus in the room.

THE BOY closes his eyes earnestly.

THE BOY

Dear Jesus … How are you? I am fine … Okay … I'm lying … What I want to know is how you feel about being the Father, Son and Holy Ghost all at once. I understand the trinity I just want to ask how you fit it all together and do you get confused? You see I am an artist. An Indian. And a Grand Shaman … It is hard for us to accept all three. I'm sure you understand … that is why I'm asking you? Hello?

THE YOUNG MAN enters carrying a tray full of booze.

THE YOUNG MAN

You're wasting your time … Hello Jesus? Anybody there … See? Nothing …

THE BOY

Dear Jesus … We've been drinking since we were thirteen years old. We get drunk often. We drink to get drunk. We don't believe in social drinking, or sipping some wine here and there. When we get drunk we want to get drunk. I've noticed we try to forget things when we get drunk but we never forget things when we get drunk because we have to live with them and we have to resolve them and we know what we're saying whether we're sober, or not.

THE YOUNG MAN and THE OLD MAN cheer each time and drink harder …

THE OLD MAN / THE YOUNG MAN

NOT!

THE BOY

But we never forget things when we get drunk … even if we want to … We have to resolve them and we know what we're saying whether we're sober or not …

THE OLD MAN / THE YOUNG MAN

NOT!

THE BOY

What is an Indian without their drink?

THE OLD MAN / THE YOUNG MAN

I said!

THE BOY

What is a Christian without their guilt?

THE OLD MAN / THE YOUNG MAN

I said!

THE BOY

What is an Indian artist?

THE OLD MAN / THE YOUNG MAN

I said!

THE BOY

I am an ARTIST and I am an INDIAN!

THE OLD MAN

There … you have it.

THE YOUNG MAN and THE OLD MAN cheer to that and all the NORVALS look up as a jail cage descends down over them.

KENORA JAIL, 1973

A light shines high in the sky like a burning sun. They all squint up and look into the light …

THE BOY

Jesus … is that you? It's me Norval …

THE OLD MAN

It's getting hot in here … you feel that …

THE OLD MAN begins to undo the buttons on his shirt.

THE BOY

Keep your clothes on … Jesus is coming …

THE YOUNG MAN

I just want a drink …

THE BOY

Jesus?

JACK appears sitting at his desk, phone in hand.

JACK

No, it's Jack …

THE YOUNG MAN

Get out of the way … it's Jack … I know how to talk to Jack … he'll get us out of here … Jack? It's me Norval …

JACK

Who? The warden from Kenora Jail. Yes … of course I know Norval Morrisseau …

THE YOUNG MAN

He's gonna tell you if you get me released from jail, I will die … That I will drink myself dehydrated … Funny that … He's lyin' Jack … It's me your brother … get me the hell out of here …

JACK looks up from his phone and over at NORVAL. They stare at each other. The heat increases …

THE YOUNG MAN

Jack please … I'm beggin' you … Ja/

JACK

/I can't do it this time Norval … I can't do you … you're killing me with your shit … and now you're killing yourself … Just stay there for a few months … make yourself better … for christsakes Norval … I've done all I can do …

THE YOUNG MAN

You've done all a white man is gonna do … that's a big fuckin' difference "brother" …

JACK

I love you Norval I just can't watch you die …

JACK in tears slowly hangs the phone up …

THE YOUNG MAN

Nobody hangs up on me Jack because I am the powerline, you hear me? … He hung up … he hung up on me … he gave up on me …

JACK buries his head on his desk. THE YOUNG MAN begins to cry with hurt and anger …

THE YOUNG MAN

Fuck you Jack … surviving makes its own family … What … you think I don't see you … You're surviving through me too … you just don't know it yet … but you will … you fuckin' will you hear me!!!

THE YOUNG MAN slides down the jail bars, crying. The heat increases …

THE OLD MAN

Shh … you're scaring the flowers …

A vision of HARRIET emerges from the brilliant sun … She floats in the sky, gathering berries and dropping them into a basket. She looks young and beautiful. THE OLD MAN smiles at her … wiping sweat from his face …

THE OLD MAN

Harriet … you shouldn't have come … or did I come to you? I went and visited my mother the other day … and left with the smell of roses … and now you … Do you think the memory of every woman has the smell of a flower, or just a man's mother? You, Harriet … you smell like blackberries … I want to collect you and put you in my mouth … I'm gonna ask you now one last time … could you save me, Harriet … pick me …

HARRIET looks up from her blackberry picking … She squints into the sun between them …

THE OLD MAN

I was thinking … If ever I had another family I will do better … I was thinking … I was thinking about taking up canning again …

They smile at the memory.

HARRIET

You have to pick the berries when they are just ripe … Pick them and put them in a basket … Don't eat too many or it will make you sick …

THE OLD MAN

Can you just give me a taste Harriet?

She picks a berry … hesitates and then places it in her mouth. The heat increases..

THE OLD MAN

My lips are so dry for something blood red … Harriet … just give me a taste for christsakes …

HARRIET

You take the most brilliant from your garden and put them in a jar and you seal your summer so nothing can get out, nothing goes to waste … you save it for long winters … long winters that seem like jail.

THE OLD MAN

I never saved nothing … not even myself for a rainy day.

HARRIET

Than what are you asking me for? You expect everyone to do the work while you eat the harvest.

THE OLD MAN

Harriet …

HARRIET turns and vanishes. THE OLD MAN squints up into the sun and slowly his legs buckle …

THE BOY excitedly yells to himselves. He climbs on the backs of his fallen selves and embraces his God descending. The heat increases …

STE. ROSE CATHOLIC DETOXIFICATION CENTRE, 1975

A grand cloaked figure descends, part human, part bird …

THE BOY

Jesus … It's Jesus … no shit … Sorry, I gotta get higher … Jesus, over here … it's me Norval … open the door …

... as it gets closer AUNTIE THE NUN comes into hovering view. Her bird headdress an exaggerated nun's habit extended outwards in flight.

AUNTIE THE NUN
It's not Jesus ... silly heathen ...

THE BOY
I'm only talkin' to Jesus 'cause he knows my pain ...

AUNTIE THE NUN
You think Jesus was an Indian?

THE BOY
He coulda been. Can you open the door? I am so afraid ... please ...

AUNTIE THE NUN
You must ask for forgiveness ...

THE BOY
For what?

THE YOUNG MAN
I have fucked everything under the sun and now I am thirsty ... Give me a drink old bird ... will you? Just a sip. Will you just this once give me a drink? I am thirsty and they have made me nothing but dry. A dry fuck. It's painful. Give me the drink now ... I said give me the drink now you Hudson's Bay taker!!!

AUNTIE THE NUN
For that ... Ask for forgiveness ... Jesus can see everything ...

THE BOY
Everything? Oh no ... not everything ... please no ... I am so afraid ... so afraid ... please ... open the door ... open the door ...

AUNTIE THE NUN
There is no door to heaven for an Indian ... but you have to have blind faith anyways ...

THE BOY begins to cry silently. The heat increases unbearably until they are all shaking with sweat ...

THE OLD MAN
In that case, can you at least get me a drink of water? I don't care who you are ... I don't care ... weird hat or not

... please ... please ... Water shouldn't be in a bottle—it gets too confusing. Tap. Tap. Tap water you ugly witch ... anything wet ... Can't you see I am hot? Can't you see my tongue is sticking ... I am so tired ...

THE YOUNG MAN

I am so lonely so Jesus lonely wandering. I am so lost, so holy lost Manitou. There is nothing but this skin cracking a broke river bed. There is nothing but empty marrow in my bones. Sucked dry by, sucked dry by, sucked dry by bear suckers and art humpers.

THE OLD MAN

I am so afraid so Jesus lonely wondering. I am so lost, so holy lost Manitou. There is nothing but this skin cracking a broke river bed. There is nothing but empty marrow in my bones. There is nothing but a fire burning in my belly.

THE BOY

You are right, I am nothing.

Silence.

AUNTIE THE NUN

You are so low it is time to ask for forgiveness. Ask for forgiveness for being yourself!

THE THREE NORVALS bend down to their knees and pray.

THE BOY

Dear God, please forgive me for being an Indian.

THE YOUNG MAN

Dear Manitou, please forgive me for being an artist.

THE OLD MAN

Dear God Manitou, please forgive me for being everything ... and not being sorry.

The sound of a fire and of burning ...

The jail cell begins to fill with brilliant colours that move and then take shape within the power line of THE YOUNG MAN, THE BOY and THE OLD MAN as they transform into characters of the Virgin Mary, Christ Child, John the Baptist, Saint Joseph, Infant Saint John, Great Mishipashoo ...

As the fire burns, the jail cell falls open and crumbles into charred pieces at their feet ... THE THREE NORVALS stand, the fire rising up their bodies.

THE THREE NORVALS

I am Norval Morrisseau. I am an artist, a storyteller. I am a mystic. I am a very religious person. I am a free man, a force. I am humble. I am Jesus Christ. I am the Creator. I am an Indian and I will save myself.

The sound of thunder.

THE THREE NORVALS raise their faces and arms upward and as they do a blue light hits their faces and hands reaching upward. They begin to ascend as Thunderbirds.

Between clouds and brilliant blue sky THE THREE NORVALS are caught in the evolution of The Man Changing into Thunderbird.

THE YOUNG MAN

My spirit becoming more than the Holy Ghost—The Thunderbird.

THE OLD MAN

My spirit becoming more than the Father—The Grand Shaman.

THE BOY

My spirit becoming more than the Son—The Artist. I am beginning to feel free.

THE HOUSE OF INVENTION

The transformation shifts into itself until they stand as three different parts of one painting.

They emerge out of the painting in threes.

THE OLD MAN walks forward as NORVAL GRAND SHAMAN.

THE YOUNG MAN walks from the painting as NORVAL THUNDERBIRD WARRIOR.

THE BOY walks from the painting as NORVAL BOY.

They look at each other and then at the room as their line extends and draws itself a power line of the Alexandria Library.

NORVAL GRAND SHAMAN

What now?

They walk forward. The NORVAL BOY nervously takes the NORVAL GRAND SHAMAN's hand. NORVAL THUNDERBIRD WARRIOR stands warrior-like.

NORVAL BOY

Where do you think we are? Some kind of hell?

NORVAL GRAND SHAMAN

It looks like some kinda wonderful to me … We are in some kind of place that lets Indians in.

NORVAL GRAND SHAMAN points to a grand round table in the centre of the room where a crystal sits on top of it. It begins to warm up and a white light blares out and forms the white-suited image of PICASSO.

NORVAL THUNDERBIRD WARRIOR

What do you want with us old bald one?

He looks at the other two.

NORVAL THUNDERBIRD WARRIOR

Should I kill him? He looks too small to kill with a good conscience.

PICASSO stands.

PICASSO

Don't let looks deceive you. I am an artist. A warrior like you … And like you I paint to make war …

NORVAL GRAND SHAMAN moves toward PICASSO.

NORVAL GRAND SHAMAN

Picasso, is that you? … When we met in Paris I said/

NORVAL THUNDERBIRD WARRIOR

/I paint to beautify the world and battle the conditioned consciousness with the same tools used to condition us/

NORVAL GRAND SHAMAN

/In this way we survive by giving life to the image of ourselves

NORVAL BOY

/We keep breathing …

PICASSO

And so you have … and so I have … despite the fires that threaten to destroy us. You are in the great Royal Library of Alexandria.

NORVAL GRAND SHAMAN

The House of Invention.

PICASSO

Breathe.

The light from the crystal begins to expand and a kaleidoscope of colour begins to blare from it and with it visible reflections of the great thinkers and artists of the world. The reflections are life-like to each personality but animated in extremely brilliant colours. Music begins and there is a collage between the personalities and their colours between the NORVAL BOY, and NORVAL THUNDERBIRD WARRIOR as they try on the colours and voices. It is noble and hip, funky and beautiful.

NORVAL THUNDERBIRD WARRIOR as BLACK ELK.

BLACK ELK

Breathing colours. One is for the heart, one is for the bum, one is for the arms, one is for all the different kinds of sicknesses …

PICASSO

It was Matisse who said "Colour goes beyond itself," and, like him, I would have to say to your selves, have good lungs.

PICASSO picks up two scrolls from the table and walks toward a podium. NORVAL GRAND SHAMAN follows. PICASSO unrolls the first scroll.

Picasso's Le Bordel *displays up.*

PICASSO

My whole life as an artist has been a continual struggle against reaction, against the death of art. When I was a young man I painted *Le Bordel,* and it is said it broke the tradition of art. An African mask helped me break hundreds of years of tradition in art. It allowed me in to look at ourselves from different angles/

NORVAL BOY walks into MARTIN LUTHER KING.

MARTIN LUTHER KING

I had a dream.

PICASSO unrolls the second scroll.

Norval Morrisseau's Serpent in Grass *line drawing displays up.*

NORVAL GRAND SHAMAN

/When I was a young man the shamans of our water and earth recorded their pictographs on the walls of caves and on the land they came from. They said to me/

NORVAL THUNDERBIRD WARRIOR walks into LEONARD COHEN.

LEONARD COHEN

The reason we exist is love.

NORVAL GRAND SHAMAN

/It is is time you knew where these images came from so you too can bring them down as great art warriors have done before you. They said/

NORVAL BOY walks into EINSTEIN.

EINSTEIN

Space and time are relative, not absolute ...

NORVAL GRAND SHAMAN

/They said ... Bring these images down and fill them with colour and in this way, heal the witnesses, and let everyone experience what it is to be Indian, what it is to love and think freely when we are artists, healers and warriors ...

Norval Morrisseau's handwriting writes, "From one great artist to another, Norval Morrisseau, Copper Thunderbird," across the displayed painting.

PICASSO

This painting you gave me in Paris and signed, "From one great artist to another," has stayed with me. Like you ... when I gave spirits form I became independent and yet connected to something more.

The walls of the library fill with images of the great masters.

PICASSO

Will you stay?

Pause.

NORVAL GRAND SHAMAN

No ... but I will paint from here ... from this knowing ...

NORVAL THE WARRIOR and NORVAL THE BOY walk toward him. NORVAL THE BOY holds NORVAL GRAND SHAMAN's hand.

THE NORVAL BOY

I want to stay here with the scrolls. I want to breathe where I can finally be everything.

NORVAL GRAND SHAMAN looks at NORVAL THUNDERBIRD WARRIOR.

NORVAL THUNDERBIRD WARRIOR

I want to stay where artists are warriors.

NORVAL BOY and NORVAL THUNDERBIRD WARRIOR look at NORVAL GRAND SHAMAN.

NORVAL GRAND SHAMAN

I was brought into this world to beautify the world with colour. To remind everyone in the end who we really are. That we are the same somewhere.

NORVAL BOY / NORVAL THUNDERBIRD WARRIOR

All connected somewhere ...

NORVAL GRAND SHAMAN

And so ...

PICASSO

Till we meet again ... Picasso of the Woods.

NORVAL GRAND SHAMAN

Till then. Morrisseau of Europe ...

NORVAL GRAND SHAMAN looks out at The House of Invention. *It is a beautiful kaleidoscope of colour. NORVAL THUNDERBIRD WARRIOR and the NORVAL BOY look at NORVAL GRAND SHAMAN as he leaves.*

LOS ANGELES, 1987

Time suspends and begins to collapse. The outlined arches of the library begin to resemble Californian hills. THE OLD MAN stands on his podium, behind him the black-outlined shape of an oval pool draws itself and fills with brilliant blue. Inside the blue, a beautiful L.A. pool girl swims across.

THE OLD MAN

... So, like I was saying. I take these images from the dream state and fill them with colour. I believe that everyone has a colour space. When one looks at a picture, the picture and the colours reflect the mind, or soul, or whatever part of the body the colour space is inside you.

Movie stars and celebrities begin to fill the gallery space chatting and stroking each other.

THE OLD MAN continues art-speaking while everyone caresses each other in a hot desert kind of Californian way. THE OLD MAN continues talking as a trio of pool girls emerge from the water, in bright bikinis, tanned and blonde, uplifted in all the right places as the exaggerated, classic CALIFORNICATION GIRLS.

THE OLD MAN

Whatever happens ... the spiritual things are what I want to put into the paintings for my people.

THE CALIFORNICATION GIRLS approach THE OLD MAN with their bossy chests.

CALIFORNICATION GIRL ONE

What colour do you think I am? My spiritual teacher "Lone Wolf On An Empty Desert" says that I inhabit a special colour.

CALIFORNICATION GIRL TWO

Do you teach yoga?

CALIFORNICATION GIRL THREE

Like ... who did you say you were?

THE OLD MAN

I am ...

THE OLD MAN stumbles as the sound of a big TV screen buzzes up. AUNTIE THE NEWSCASTER enters the screen in ultimate TV anchor attire.

THE OLD MAN looks at her and then back at the gallery-goers. He tries to stay on track.

AUNTIE THE NEWSCASTER

Norval Morrisseau ...

THE OLD MAN

I am Norval Morrisseau/

AUNTIE THE NEWSCASTER

/a well-known bullheaded Canadian artist is wandering the downtown streets, sleeping in parks and alleys and selling sketches for the price of a bottle of liquor.

THE OLD MAN

I have the Indian name of ...

AUNTIE THE NEWSCASTER

Has been./

THE OLD MAN

/Copper Thunderbird! I am ...

AUNTIE THE NEWSCASTER

/a useless savage!!

THE OLD MAN

I am a born ...

AUNTIE THE NEWSCASTER

/Drunk who didn't get a trade.

THE OLD MAN

I am a born artist. A born ARTIST!

THE OLD MAN

Could someone get me a drink of water? I'm getting stuck ...

CALIFORNICATION GIRL ONE grabs a bottle of tequila and hands it to him. THE OLD MAN tries to protest but is silenced by her demands ...

THE OLD MAN

I don't drink ...

CALIFORNICATION GIRL ONE

A real Indian, imagine that girls ... wow ... What's it like being an Indian, Norval? Like is it exciting?

CALIFORNICATION GIRL THREE

Like seriously ... I just have to ask you ... did you like *Dances with Wolves*? Or did you think it exploited the struggles of Indians everywhere ... because like there's always a white chick that gets to be an Indian.

CALIFORNICATION GIRL TWO

Like personally, I watch that and all I can see is Kevin Costner's great ass and one smart wolf. Do you like my ass?

CALIFORNICATION GIRL ONE

Do you have a wolf?

THE OLD MAN looks at the vacant faces of THE CALIFORNICATION GIRLS, he looks at the bottle in his hand, he looks at the TV screen where AUNTIE THE NEWSCASTER begins to interview the THREE DUMP BEARS. They jockey for position.

AUNTIE THE NEWSCASTER

Today, we have the rare opportunity to talk with three of Mr. Morrisseau's closest friends/

DUMP BEAR ONE taps her on the shoulder and whispers into her ear.

AUNTIE THE NEWSCASTER

I'm sorry ... colleagues of Mr. Morrisseau ... Thank you gentlemen for being with us here today ...

DUMP BEAR ONE

Thank you ... As a close close friend of Mr. Morrisseau and a fellow artist with my own body of work ... it pains me to say that many of Mr. Morrisseau's latest works are actually mine ... I wasn't going to say anything but since you asked ...

DUMP BEAR TWO

He would say "sell them," "sell them" and "let's drink" ... pitiful really ... So I bought them from him for ten bucks as a favour ... they are worth thousands of dollars now ...

DUMP BEAR THREE

Besides he's a homosexual anyways ...

THE OLD MAN looks at THE DUMP BEARS sadly.

THE OLD MAN

Shut up ... shut up ... you small town garbage eaters.

CALIFORNICATION GIRL THREE

Norval, it looks like you are sad ... are you sad? Because I get sad somedays ...

THE OLD MAN

I wanted to believe inside we are all the same somewhere.

CALIFORNICATION GIRL TWO

That's exactly what I think ... we're all the same somewhere ... we've all been fucked ... you know what I mean?

THE OLD MAN

I wish I could die. I'd die on the street. I don't care because I would be free from this ... I'd be gone ... free ... goodbye body ...

CALIFORNICATION GIRL THREE

I wish I could die too ... me too ...

CALIFORNICATION GIRL ONE

Me too ...

CALIFORNICATION GIRL TWO

Me too ... weird ...

THE OLD MAN looks at them.

CALIFORNICATION GIRL TWO

/Because I for one am tired of being objectified as a blonde with big porcelain tits and I want to know if you feel the same way being an Indian. Norval?

CALIFORNICATION GIRL ONE

Norval, she's talking to you ...

They look at each other.

CALIFORNICATION GIRL THREE

Rude.

THE OLD MAN brings the bottle closer to his lips. He looks at a worm floating at the bottom.

THE OLD MAN

I'm talking to you, snake ... you have changed form but I can see you ... Smaller like the worm you are.

CALIFORNICATION GIRL TWO

I'm sorry?

THE OLD MAN

I said, are your tits so big you can't hear?

CALIFORNICATION GIRL ONE

She's talking about something important here.

CALIFORNICATION GIRL TWO begins to cry

THE OLD MAN

I don't give a fuck! I was trying to talk about art. I was trying to talk about something real!/

CALIFORNICATION GIRL TWO

My tits are real ... and nobody ... Nobody has *not* wanted to talk about my tits!

She leaves crying and the other two CALIFORNICATION GIRLS follow her trying to console her as they are intercepted by AUNTIE THE NEWSCASTER.

AUNTIE THE NEWSCASTER

Excuse me young ladies ... You look ... disturbed ... Given your intimate relationships with Mr. Morrisseau, and for the information of our viewers could you give us your honest opinion of the great artist?

CALIFORNICATION GIRL ONE

I think he's one of the saddest people you could ever wish to see. I mean he looks God awful.

CALIFORNICATION GIRL TWO

I feel like I want to help him ... you know what I mean ... but any money you give him goes straight to ... liquor.

THE OLD MAN

Any money they give you goes straight to your tits!

THE OLD MAN looks at the bottle of tequila and then begins to guzzle it.

The THREE DUMP BEARS in L.A. shout ...

THE THREE L.A. DUMP BEARS

TEQUILA!!!!!!

The DUMP BEARS go into a Tequila Dance. They grab THE OLD MAN and raise him above their shoulders dancing, the crowd following behind.

AUNTIE THE NEWSCASTER

Today, Mr. Morrisseau makes about forty dollars a day selling his sketches on the streets.

They throw him and he lands on the bed in his room. As he lands he struggles to get up and then sits on the edge of his bed ...

Norval Morrisseau appears as a live newspaper article in his Vancouver downtown eastside hotel sitting on the edge of his bed, disheveled, bloated and alone.

AUNTIE THE NEWSCASTER

A huge fall for Mr. Morrisseau who had come to be known as The Father of Contemporary Indian Art, his work included in prestigious exhibitions in Chicago, New York, Montreal and Paris …

The caption reads: "DRINK OF TEQUILA STARTED PAINTER ON ROAD TO DESPAIR."

And below his picture: "CANADIAN ARTIST NORVAL MORRISSEAU IS SELLING SKETCHES IN VANCOUVER TO BUY LIQUOR. VANCOUVER, 1987."

AUNTIE THE NEWSCASTER

The Ojibway boy painter in the woods who had a vision of greatness when a bear whispered in his ears is now living a reality all too familiar for his kind on the rainy skid row streets of Vancouver … I told you so.

He finally looks at the sky of his room that becomes light blue, and moving clouds. He leans over and picks up a pencil and paper from his bedside and he draws a circle, a circle is drawn and hollowed in the sky. A mauve light flows from the circle, above to below, and with it the appearance and mauve voice of NORVAL KATERI. THE OLD MAN smiles.

As she speaks from above, NORVAL THUNDERBIRD WARRIOR appears with THE NORVAL BOY at the opening of the circle, they stand between worlds and then continue walking downwards in the mauve toward THE OLD MAN.

NORVAL KATERI

You remember you painted the story of me. The story of Kateri, Lily of the Mohawks … And in your picture story of me my face was not scarred with small pox … I was still beautiful, unscarred by the diseases of white men and our own history making. So I ask you, do your scars matter when we can see each other's soul?

NORVAL THUNDERBIRD WARRIOR and NORVAL BOY reach THE OLD MAN and kiss him like a grandfather …

They look at the sand that has turned to ornamen red and where Norval lilies begin to rise from the red sand and grow into great orchards of limbs and blooms.

From above another Norval baby boy, and another Norval baby girl, descend down and another Norval Man and another Norval Woman descend down etc., increasingly taking their place among the great family tree of limbs and lilies and Indians.

NORVAL KATERI

You have to remember you have given everything you are … You have to remember you have given acres and acres of being Indian … Even with our scars … do we not deserve love? Can we not be beautiful? We all have scars where the lilies grow …

The sound of the tide rising.

Behind we see the imprint of Norval Morrisseau's signature on the right hand corner of this canvas.

The Norval boys, girls, women and men, grandfathers and grandmothers, artists and shamans leave the canvas and walk toward THE THREE NORVALS standing behind them.

THE OLD MAN / THE BOY / THE YOUNG MAN

I am Norval Morrisseau …

THE CANVAS

We are Norval Morrisseau.

THE OLD MAN

I drew and if the water came and washed it away that's the way the saga goes … or does it?

THE OLD MAN laughs.

The sound of the tide rising increases …

THE NORVAL BOY steps forward knee deep in blue. He stops and looks back.

THE NORVAL BOY

Are you coming or not?

THE OLD MAN

What do we have to fear?

THE OLD MAN laughs.

NORVAL THUNDERBIRD WARRIOR takes THE OLD MAN's hand as they follow THE NORVAL BOY into the water. The other Norvals do the same. They all step forward and watch as a giant blue wave approaches and submerges them in the depth of his blues.

Blue out.